Table of Contents

Table of Contents 1

Introduction: Exploring the Concept of Soul Murder 3

Chapter 1: The Anatomy of Organizational Trauma .. 7

Chapter 2: Unmasking Toxic Cultures: Signs and Symptoms 11

Chapter 3: Betrayal and Broken Trust: The Core of Soul Murder 16

Chapter 4: Power Dynamics and Their Impact on Workplace Dynamics 20

Chapter 5: The Psychology of Soul Murder: How it Affects Individuals 26

Chapter 6: Coping Mechanisms: Survival Strategies in Toxic Environments 32

Chapter 7: Healing Wounds: Strategies for Recovery and Resilience 37

Chapter 8: Breaking the Cycle: Transforming Organizational Culture 42

Chapter 9: Holding Accountable: Addressing Perpetrators and Enablers 47

Chapter 10: Building Support Networks: Finding Allies in Healing 53

Reclaiming Power: A Case Study of Overcoming
Organizational Soul Murder 62

Conclusion: Towards a Future of Wholeness and
Well-being 67

Introduction: Exploring the Concept of Soul Murder

In the vast landscape of workplace dynamics, there exists a realm of experiences that transcends the ordinary challenges of professional life. This realm, often hidden beneath the surface of organizational structures and corporate jargon, is where the concept of "soul murder" finds its unsettling home. Soul murder in the workplace represents a profound betrayal of the human spirit, where individuals are subjected to conditions that corrode their sense of self, diminish their dignity, and erode their capacity to flourish.

The Origins of Soul Murder

The term "soul murder" was coined by the psychoanalyst Leonard Shengold in his seminal work "Soul Murder: The Effects of Childhood Abuse and Deprivation." Shengold used this term to describe the profound psychological harm inflicted on individuals who experienced severe neglect, abuse, or trauma during childhood. Over time, the concept has expanded beyond its original context to encompass a broader range of experiences, including those that occur in the crucible of the workplace.

Defining Soul Murder in the Workplace

Soul murder in the workplace can take many forms, ranging from overt acts of cruelty and exploitation to subtle forms of psychological manipulation and emotional abuse. At its core, soul murder is characterized by the systematic dehumanization of individuals within the organizational context. It is the erosion of one's sense of worth, agency, and belonging in the pursuit of organizational goals or the gratification of those in positions of power.

Understanding the Impact

The consequences of soul murder in the workplace are profound and far-reaching. For those who are its victims, the experience can be akin to a slow, agonizing death of the spirit. It manifests in feelings of powerlessness, despair, and existential alienation. It can lead to a pervasive sense of emptiness and meaninglessness that permeates every aspect of one's life. Moreover, the effects of soul murder extend beyond the individual, creating ripple effects that undermine the collective well-being of teams, departments, and entire organizations.

Exploring the Dynamics

To understand soul murder in the workplace, we must delve into the complex interplay of psychological, social, and organizational factors that give rise to it. At its core, soul murder is often facilitated by environments characterized by toxic power dynamics, unchecked authoritarianism, and a culture of silence and complicity. It thrives in environments where individuals are objectified, exploited, and dehumanized for the sake of profit, prestige, or power.

The Importance of Recognition

One of the greatest challenges in addressing soul murder in the workplace is the pervasive culture of denial and normalization that surrounds it. Too often, the signs and symptoms of soul murder are dismissed or rationalized as simply the inevitable byproducts of competitive business environments or high-stress industries. However, to ignore or minimize the reality of soul murder is to perpetuate the harm it inflicts and to perpetuate a cycle of suffering and dysfunction.

The Promise of Healing

Despite its devastating impact, soul murder is not an inevitability. With awareness, compassion, and concerted effort, it is possible to create workplaces that nurture the human spirit rather than crush it. This book is an exploration of that promise—a journey into the heart of darkness that exists within some workplaces, but also a beacon of hope for those who seek to reclaim their dignity, their humanity, and their souls.

In the chapters that follow, we will delve deeper into the various dimensions of soul murder in the workplace, examining its causes, its consequences, and its antidotes. We will explore the stories of those who have experienced soul murder firsthand and the strategies they have employed to heal and rebuild their lives. And, most importantly, we will chart a course towards a future where the workplace is not a site of soul murder, but a sanctuary for the flourishing of the human spirit.

Chapter 1: The Anatomy of Organizational Trauma

In the intricate ecosystem of the workplace, trauma can take on many forms, ranging from isolated incidents of mistreatment to systemic patterns of abuse. Organizational trauma, however, represents a distinct category—a collective wound that permeates the very fabric of an organization, leaving lasting scars on its members and impacting its culture, productivity, and sustainability. In this chapter, we will dissect the anatomy of organizational trauma, exploring its origins, manifestations, and implications for individuals and institutions alike.

Origins of Organizational Trauma

Organizational trauma often has its roots in systemic dysfunction, structural inequalities, and toxic cultures that prioritize profit over people and power over principles. It may be triggered by events such as mass layoffs, corporate scandals, or instances of workplace violence, but its effects are often cumulative, stemming from years of neglect, mismanagement, and institutionalized abuse. Moreover, organizational trauma can be perpetuated by leaders who prioritize their own agendas over the well-being of their employees, creating a cycle of toxicity that is difficult to break.

Manifestations of Trauma

The symptoms of organizational trauma are as varied as they are insidious, manifesting in behaviors, attitudes, and patterns of interaction that undermine trust, collaboration, and morale. Employees may experience heightened levels of stress, anxiety, and burnout, leading to decreased productivity, absenteeism, and turnover. They may exhibit symptoms of post-traumatic stress disorder (PTSD), such as hypervigilance, flashbacks, and emotional numbing, in response to triggers that remind them of past traumas. Moreover, organizational trauma can lead to a breakdown in communication, conflict escalation, and a culture of blame and retaliation that further exacerbates the harm.

Impact on Individuals

For individuals who are directly affected by organizational trauma, the consequences can be devastating. They may experience a profound sense of betrayal, disillusionment, and loss of purpose as their trust in the organization and its leaders is shattered. Their self-esteem and self-efficacy may be eroded, leading to feelings of worthlessness and inadequacy that pervade every aspect of their lives. Moreover, the psychological toll of organizational trauma can spill over into other domains, affecting relationships, health, and overall well-being.

Impact on Organizations

The impact of organizational trauma is not limited to its individual victims—it reverberates throughout the entire organization, undermining its ability to function effectively and sustainably. Trust, which is the bedrock of healthy organizational cultures, is eroded, leading to increased conflict, turnover, and disengagement among employees. Productivity and innovation suffer as resources are diverted towards managing the fallout from trauma rather than towards achieving the organization's mission and goals. Moreover, organizational trauma can tarnish the organization's reputation, leading to a loss of credibility and trust among stakeholders, including customers, investors, and the broader community.

Healing Organizational Trauma

Healing organizational trauma requires a multifaceted approach that addresses its underlying causes, mitigates its immediate effects, and fosters resilience and growth within the organization. This process begins with acknowledging the reality of trauma and its impact on individuals and the organization as a whole. It involves creating a culture of transparency, accountability, and psychological safety where employees feel empowered to speak out against injustice and to seek support when needed. Moreover, healing organizational trauma requires leadership that is committed to fostering a culture of compassion, empathy, and respect, where the well-being of employees is prioritized over short-term profits or personal agendas.

Conclusion

Organizational trauma is a pervasive and pernicious force that can wreak havoc on individuals, organizations, and communities. Its effects are far-reaching and long-lasting, undermining trust, productivity, and well-being. However, by understanding the anatomy of organizational trauma and committing to its healing and prevention, we can create workplaces that are resilient, compassionate, and just. In the chapters that follow, we will explore the strategies and interventions that can help organizations confront and overcome the legacy of trauma, creating a future where workplaces are not sites of suffering, but sources of strength and fulfillment for all who inhabit them.

Chapter 2: Unmasking Toxic Cultures: Signs and Symptoms

Within every organization, there exists a culture—a set of shared beliefs, values, and norms that shape the behavior and interactions of its members. While a healthy organizational culture can foster collaboration, innovation, and employee well-being, a toxic culture can have the opposite effect, creating an environment that is rife with dysfunction, conflict, and suffering. In this chapter, we will unmask the signs and symptoms of toxic cultures, shedding light on the hidden dynamics that perpetuate harm and undermine organizational health.

Understanding Toxic Cultures

Toxic cultures are characterized by a pervasive pattern of dysfunction and pathology that undermines trust, collaboration, and morale within the organization. They may be fueled by a variety of factors, including poor leadership, inadequate communication, and a lack of accountability. Moreover, toxic cultures often prioritize short-term goals and individual interests over the long-term well-being of employees and the organization as a whole. As a result, they can perpetuate a cycle of toxicity that is difficult to break without concerted effort and intervention.

Signs of Toxic Cultures

1. Authoritarian Leadership: In toxic cultures, power is concentrated in the hands of a few individuals who wield it to exert control and dominance over others. Decisions are made unilaterally, without input or feedback from those affected by them, leading to feelings of powerlessness and resentment among employees.

2. Lack of Transparency: Toxic cultures are often characterized by a lack of transparency and openness, where information is hoarded and decisions are made behind closed doors. This lack of transparency breeds mistrust and suspicion among employees, who may feel as though they are being kept in the dark about important issues affecting their work and their livelihoods.

3. Fear-Based Management: In toxic cultures, fear is used as a tool to motivate and control employees, rather than trust, respect, or intrinsic motivation. Employees may be subjected to threats, intimidation, and bullying tactics if they fail to meet unrealistic expectations or challenge the status quo.

4. High Turnover Rates: Toxic cultures tend to have higher rates of turnover as employees become disillusioned and disengaged with their work environment. This constant churn can create instability and disrupt productivity, as new employees

must be recruited, onboarded, and trained to replace those who have left.

5. Micromanagement: In toxic cultures, micromanagement is often the norm rather than the exception. Employees may be subjected to constant scrutiny and oversight, with little autonomy or freedom to make decisions or take ownership of their work. This lack of trust can stifle creativity and innovation, leading to stagnation and complacency within the organization.

6. Lack of Diversity and Inclusion: Toxic cultures often lack diversity and inclusion, perpetuating systems of privilege and oppression that marginalize certain groups of employees. This lack of diversity can lead to homogeneity of thought and perspective, inhibiting creativity, innovation, and adaptability within the organization.

Symptoms of Toxic Cultures

1. Low Morale: Employees in toxic cultures often experience low morale and job satisfaction, as their contributions are undervalued and their voices go unheard. This lack of motivation can lead to decreased productivity, absenteeism, and turnover, as employees become disengaged and disillusioned with their work environment.

2. High Levels of Stress: Toxic cultures are often characterized by high levels of stress and burnout among employees, as they struggle to meet unrealistic expectations and navigate a hostile work environment. This chronic stress can take a toll on physical and mental health, leading to a range of health problems, including anxiety, depression, and cardiovascular disease.

3. Increased Conflict: Toxic cultures tend to breed conflict and hostility among employees, as they compete for limited resources and vie for recognition and advancement. This conflict can manifest in interpersonal conflicts, passive-aggressive behavior, and sabotage, further undermining trust and cohesion within the organization.

4. Lack of Innovation: In toxic cultures, innovation is often stifled as employees become hesitant to take risks or think outside the box. This fear of failure and reprisal can inhibit creativity and experimentation, leading to stagnation and missed opportunities for growth and innovation.

5. Poor Performance: Ultimately, toxic cultures tend to result in poor performance and outcomes for the organization, as employees become demoralized and disengaged with their work. This can manifest in missed deadlines, quality issues, and decreased

customer satisfaction, as employees struggle to meet the demands of a dysfunctional work environment.

Conclusion

Unmasking toxic cultures requires a willingness to confront uncomfortable truths and challenge entrenched power dynamics within the organization. It requires leadership that is committed to fostering a culture of trust, transparency, and accountability, where employees feel valued, respected, and empowered to speak out against injustice and abuse. Moreover, it requires a collective effort from all members of the organization to recognize the signs and symptoms of toxicity and work together to create a healthier, more inclusive work environment for everyone. In the chapters that follow, we will explore strategies and interventions for addressing toxic cultures and fostering a culture of well-being, resilience, and growth within the organization.

Chapter 3: Betrayal and Broken Trust: The Core of Soul Murder

In the intricate tapestry of human relationships, trust serves as the foundation upon which all meaningful connections are built. It is the glue that binds individuals together, fostering a sense of safety, security, and mutual respect. However, when trust is violated, when promises are broken, and when betrayal occurs, the repercussions can be profound and far-reaching. In the context of the workplace, betrayal and broken trust lie at the heart of soul murder, eroding the very essence of what it means to be human and inflicting deep wounds on the psyche of individuals and organizations alike.

Understanding Betrayal

Betrayal is a multifaceted phenomenon that can take many forms, ranging from overt acts of deception and disloyalty to more subtle forms of breach of trust and abandonment. It may occur at the hands of colleagues, supervisors, or the organization itself, and its impact can be devastating for those who experience it. Betrayal undermines the fundamental assumptions upon which relationships are based, leading to feelings of anger, sadness, and disillusionment as individuals grapple with the painful reality of broken trust.

The Dynamics of Broken Trust

Broken trust often occurs in the context of power imbalances and unequal relationships within the workplace. Employees may be promised opportunities for advancement, recognition, or fair treatment, only to have those promises broken or reneged upon. They may be subjected to unfair treatment, favoritism, or discrimination based on factors such as race, gender, or social status. Moreover, broken trust can occur at the interpersonal level, as colleagues betray confidences, spread rumors, or engage in backstabbing behavior that undermines relationships and erodes trust.

The Impact of Betrayal

The impact of betrayal in the workplace is profound and far-reaching, affecting not only the individuals directly involved but also the broader organizational culture and dynamics. For those who experience betrayal firsthand, the consequences can be devastating. They may experience a loss of faith in themselves, in others, and in the organization as a whole, leading to feelings of betrayal and disillusionment that pervade every aspect of their work and their lives. Moreover, the psychological toll of betrayal can manifest in a range of symptoms, including anxiety, depression, and post-traumatic stress disorder (PTSD), as individuals struggle to make sense of their experiences and find a way forward.

Betrayal and Organizational Culture

Betrayal and broken trust are often symptomatic of deeper issues within the organizational culture, including a lack of transparency, accountability, and integrity. In organizations where trust is not valued or prioritized, betrayal can become the norm rather than the exception, leading to a culture of cynicism, resentment, and disengagement among employees. Moreover, the erosion of trust can have serious implications for organizational performance and effectiveness, as employees become hesitant to collaborate, share information, or take risks in pursuit of common goals.

Healing Broken Trust

Healing broken trust requires a concerted effort from both individuals and organizations to acknowledge the harm that has been done and to work together towards reconciliation and restoration. This process begins with a willingness to confront uncomfortable truths and to take responsibility for one's actions and their impact on others. It involves creating a culture of accountability, transparency, and open communication where grievances can be aired, grievances addressed, and trust rebuilt over time. Moreover, healing broken trust requires leadership that is committed to fostering a culture of integrity, respect, and fairness, where the well-being of employees is prioritized over short-term gains or personal agendas.

Conclusion

Betrayal and broken trust lie at the core of soul murder in the workplace, eroding the very foundations upon which healthy organizations are built. However, by understanding the dynamics of betrayal, acknowledging its impact, and committing to healing and reconciliation, it is possible to create workplaces where trust is valued, respected, and nurtured. In the chapters that follow, we will explore strategies and interventions for addressing betrayal and broken trust in the workplace and fostering a culture of integrity, respect, and collaboration for all who inhabit it.

Chapter 4: Power Dynamics and Their Impact on Workplace Dynamics

In every workplace, power dynamics play a crucial role in shaping relationships, decision-making processes, and overall organizational culture. Power, in its various forms, influences how individuals interact with one another, how conflicts are resolved, and who holds sway over key resources and opportunities. However, when power is wielded inappropriately or abused, it can lead to a host of negative consequences, including discrimination, harassment, and the erosion of trust and morale. In this chapter, we will explore the complex interplay of power dynamics in the workplace and their profound impact on organizational dynamics and employee well-being.

Understanding Power Dynamics

Power can be conceptualized in many ways, ranging from formal authority granted by organizational hierarchy to informal influence derived from expertise, charisma, or social connections. It can manifest in overt displays of dominance and control, such as micromanagement and intimidation, or in more subtle forms of coercion and manipulation. Moreover, power dynamics are often influenced by factors such as race, gender, age, and socioeconomic status, creating hierarchies of privilege and oppression that shape the experiences of individuals within the organization.

Types of Power

Power in the workplace can be classified into several distinct types, each with its own dynamics and implications for organizational dynamics:

Positional Power: Positional power is derived from one's formal authority within the organization, such as managers, supervisors, and executives. Those in positions of authority have the ability to make decisions, allocate resources, and enforce policies, giving them significant influence over the actions and behaviors of subordinates.

Expert Power: Expert power is based on one's knowledge, skills, and expertise in a particular domain. Individuals who possess expert power are often sought out for their advice, guidance, and insights, making them influential figures within the organization, regardless of their formal position or title.

Referent Power: Referent power is derived from one's personal charisma, likability, and influence over others. Individuals who possess referent power are often seen as role models or mentors within the organization, and their opinions and actions carry weight with their colleagues and peers.

Coercive Power: Coercive power is based on the ability to punish or withhold rewards from others. It may involve threats, intimidation, or other forms of negative reinforcement to compel compliance or obedience from subordinates.

Reward Power: Reward power is based on the ability to provide incentives or benefits to others in exchange for compliance or cooperation. It may involve offering promotions, raises, or other forms of recognition to motivate employees to achieve desired outcomes.

Impact of Power Dynamics

Power dynamics can have a profound impact on workplace dynamics, shaping the behavior and interactions of individuals within the organization. When power is wielded fairly and responsibly, it can foster collaboration, innovation, and mutual respect among employees. However, when power is abused or misused, it can lead to a host of negative consequences, including:

Abuse of Authority: Individuals in positions of power may abuse their authority to exploit or manipulate others for personal gain. This can lead to feelings of resentment, disillusionment, and distrust among employees, as they struggle to navigate a hostile work environment where their well-being is not prioritized.

Discrimination and Harassment: Power dynamics can create fertile ground for discrimination and harassment, particularly when those in positions of power use their influence to perpetuate systems of privilege and oppression. This can manifest in various forms, including unequal treatment, favoritism, and exclusion based on factors such as race, gender, or sexual orientation.

Erosion of Trust: When power is wielded unfairly or arbitrarily, it can erode trust and undermine the integrity of the organization. Employees may become hesitant to speak out against injustice or report misconduct for fear of retaliation or reprisal, further perpetuating a culture of silence and complicity within the organization.

Decreased Morale and Productivity: Power dynamics can create a toxic work environment characterized by low morale, high turnover, and decreased productivity. When employees feel powerless or marginalized, they may become disengaged and demotivated, leading to decreased performance and increased absenteeism.

Stifled Innovation: In environments where power is concentrated in the hands of a few individuals, innovation and creativity may be stifled as employees become hesitant to challenge the status quo or take risks. This can result in missed opportunities for growth and innovation, as the organization becomes stagnant and resistant to change.

Addressing Power Imbalances

Addressing power imbalances in the workplace requires a multifaceted approach that involves both structural and cultural interventions. It begins with creating policies and procedures that promote fairness, transparency, and accountability in decision-making processes. It also involves fostering a culture of respect, inclusivity, and empowerment, where all employees feel valued, respected, and heard, regardless of their position or status within the organization. Moreover, addressing power imbalances requires leadership that is committed to modeling ethical behavior and holding others accountable for their actions, creating a culture of integrity and trust that permeates every level of the organization.

Conclusion

Power dynamics are an inherent aspect of workplace dynamics, shaping the behavior and interactions of individuals within the organization. When wielded responsibly, power can foster collaboration, innovation, and mutual respect among employees.

However, when abused or misused, it can lead to a host of negative consequences, including discrimination, harassment, and the erosion of trust and morale. By understanding the complex interplay of power dynamics in the workplace and taking proactive steps to address power imbalances, organizations can create a culture of fairness, transparency, and accountability that promotes the well-being and success of all who inhabit it. In the chapters that follow, we will explore strategies and interventions for addressing power dynamics and fostering a culture of equity, inclusion, and empowerment within the organization.

Chapter 5: The Psychology of Soul Murder: How it Affects Individuals

Within the context of the workplace, soul murder represents a profound betrayal of the human spirit, leaving individuals feeling stripped of their dignity, agency, and sense of self-worth. The psychological impact of soul murder is far-reaching, affecting not only the individual who experiences it but also their relationships, their well-being, and their overall quality of life. In this chapter, we will explore the psychological dynamics of soul murder, examining how it affects individuals and the strategies they employ to cope with and overcome its devastating effects.

Understanding Soul Murder

Soul murder in the workplace occurs when individuals are subjected to conditions that dehumanize, objectify, or exploit them for the sake of organizational goals or the gratification of those in positions of power. It may involve overt acts of cruelty and abuse, such as harassment, discrimination, or exploitation, or more subtle forms of psychological manipulation and emotional coercion. Regardless of its form, soul murder represents a violation of the fundamental principles of dignity, respect, and human rights, leaving individuals feeling powerless, disempowered, and disconnected from their own humanity.

The Psychological Impact

The psychological impact of soul murder can be profound and far-reaching, affecting every aspect of an individual's life. At its core, soul murder represents a betrayal of trust—an experience that shakes the very foundations upon which healthy relationships and self-esteem are built. Individuals who experience soul murder may struggle with a range of emotional and psychological symptoms, including:

Loss of Trust: Soul murder undermines the individual's trust in themselves, in others, and in the fairness and integrity of the organization. They may become hyper-vigilant, suspicious, and guarded in their interactions with others, fearing further betrayal or exploitation.

Feelings of Worthlessness: Soul murder erodes the individual's sense of self-worth and self-esteem, leaving them feeling inadequate, worthless, and undeserving of love and respect. They may internalize the negative messages and stereotypes perpetuated by their abusers, leading to feelings of shame, guilt, and self-blame.

Emotional Numbing: In response to the trauma of soul murder, individuals may experience emotional numbing—a dissociative state in which they feel disconnected from their emotions and their sense of self. They may struggle to identify or express their feelings, leading to a sense of emptiness and detachment from themselves and others.

Anxiety and Depression: Soul murder can lead to heightened levels of anxiety and depression as individuals struggle to cope with the overwhelming feelings of powerlessness, hopelessness, and despair. They may experience intrusive thoughts, flashbacks, and nightmares related to their traumatic experiences, further exacerbating their distress.

Loss of Identity: Soul murder can erode the individual's sense of identity and autonomy, leaving them feeling like a shell of their former selves. They may struggle to assert their needs and boundaries, feeling as though they have lost control over their own lives and destinies.

Coping Mechanisms

In the face of soul murder, individuals may employ a variety of coping mechanisms to manage their distress and regain a sense of control over their lives. These coping mechanisms may include:

Denial and Avoidance: Individuals may attempt to cope with the trauma of soul murder by denying or minimizing its impact on their lives. They may avoid confronting painful memories or emotions, numbing themselves to the reality of their experiences in an effort to protect themselves from further harm.

Hyper-Vigilance: In response to the trauma of soul murder, individuals may become hyper-vigilant, constantly scanning their environment for signs of danger or threat. They may struggle to relax or let their guard down, fearing that they will be betrayed or exploited once again.

Social Withdrawal: Individuals who have experienced soul murder may withdraw from social interactions, isolating themselves from others as a means of self-protection. They may struggle to trust or connect with others, fearing that they will be hurt or betrayed once again.

Seeking Support: Despite the challenges they face, individuals who have experienced soul murder may seek out support from trusted friends, family members, or mental health professionals. They may find solace in sharing their experiences with others who have undergone similar traumas, finding validation and empathy in their shared struggles.

Healing and Recovery

Healing from soul murder requires a multifaceted approach that addresses the psychological, emotional, and spiritual dimensions of the individual's experience. It involves acknowledging the reality of the trauma and its impact on the individual's life, as well as validating their feelings and experiences. It also involves fostering a sense of empowerment and agency, helping the individual reclaim their sense of self-worth, dignity, and autonomy.

Conclusion

The psychological impact of soul murder in the workplace is profound and far-reaching, affecting every aspect of an individual's life. However, by understanding the psychological dynamics of soul murder and the strategies individuals employ to cope with and overcome its devastating effects, we can create a future where workplaces are not sites of suffering, but sources of strength and resilience for all who inhabit them. In the chapters that follow, we will explore strategies and interventions for healing and recovery from soul murder, fostering a culture of empathy, compassion, and justice within the organization.

Chapter 6: Coping Mechanisms: Survival Strategies in Toxic Environments

In the crucible of a toxic workplace, individuals are often forced to confront a myriad of challenges that threaten their well-being and sanity. From abusive bosses to toxic colleagues, the pressures of navigating a hostile work environment can take a toll on even the most resilient of individuals. In this chapter, we will explore the coping mechanisms that individuals employ to survive and thrive in toxic environments, examining both adaptive and maladaptive strategies and their implications for mental health and well-being.

Understanding Coping Mechanisms

Coping mechanisms are the psychological strategies and behaviors that individuals use to manage stress, regulate emotions, and adapt to challenging situations. In the context of a toxic workplace, coping mechanisms play a crucial role in helping individuals navigate the myriad of stressors and threats to their well-being. However, not all coping mechanisms are created equal—while some may promote resilience and adaptive functioning, others may contribute to further distress and dysfunction.

Adaptive Coping Mechanisms

Seeking Social Support: One of the most effective coping mechanisms in toxic environments is seeking support from trusted friends, family members, or colleagues. Having a supportive network of individuals who validate and empathize with one's experiences can provide a buffer against the negative effects of workplace stress and help individuals feel less isolated and alone.

Setting Boundaries: Setting clear boundaries is essential for protecting one's physical and emotional well-being in toxic environments. This may involve saying no to unreasonable demands, delegating tasks, or taking breaks when needed to recharge and replenish one's energy.

Self-Care Practices: Engaging in self-care practices such as exercise, meditation, and mindfulness can help individuals manage stress and promote overall well-being. Taking time to prioritize one's physical and mental health is essential for maintaining resilience and coping with the demands of a toxic workplace.

Seeking Professional Help: In some cases, coping with the stress of a toxic workplace may require the support of a mental health professional. Therapy or counseling can provide individuals with the tools and strategies they need to manage their emotions, navigate difficult relationships, and develop healthy coping mechanisms.

Maladaptive Coping Mechanisms

Avoidance: Avoidance is a common coping mechanism in toxic environments, where individuals may attempt to escape or avoid stressful situations rather than confront them directly. While avoidance may provide temporary relief, it ultimately prevents individuals from addressing the root causes of their distress and can lead to further dysfunction and distress.

Substance Abuse: Some individuals may turn to alcohol, drugs, or other substances as a way to cope with the stress of a toxic workplace. While substance abuse may provide temporary relief from emotional pain, it ultimately exacerbates the problem and can lead to addiction, health problems, and further impairment in functioning.

Passive Aggression: In environments where direct confrontation is discouraged or punished, individuals may resort to passive-aggressive behaviors as a way to express their frustrations and assert their autonomy. While passive aggression may provide a sense of control in the short term, it ultimately undermines trust and communication within the organization, leading to further conflict and dysfunction.

Emotional Detachment: Emotional detachment is another common coping mechanism in toxic environments, where individuals may shut down emotionally in order to protect themselves from further harm. While emotional detachment may provide a temporary reprieve from painful emotions, it ultimately prevents individuals from forming meaningful connections with others and can lead to feelings of loneliness and isolation.

Cultivating Resilience

Ultimately, coping with the stress of a toxic workplace requires cultivating resilience—the ability to bounce back from adversity and thrive in the face of challenges. This involves developing a repertoire of adaptive coping strategies, building a supportive network of relationships, and fostering a sense of self-efficacy and optimism in the face of adversity. By cultivating resilience, individuals can weather the storms of a toxic workplace with grace and dignity, emerging stronger and more resilient in the process.

Conclusion

Coping with the stress of a toxic workplace is a formidable challenge that requires individuals to draw on their inner resources and resilience. By understanding the coping mechanisms that individuals employ to navigate toxic environments, we can better support those who are struggling and create a culture of compassion and empathy within the organization. In the chapters that follow, we will explore strategies and interventions for promoting resilience and well-being in toxic workplaces, fostering a culture of support, and empowerment for all who inhabit it.

Chapter 7: Healing Wounds: Strategies for Recovery and Resilience

In the aftermath of experiencing soul murder in the workplace, individuals are left grappling with deep wounds that can impact every aspect of their lives. Healing from the trauma of a toxic work environment requires a multifaceted approach that addresses the emotional, psychological, and spiritual dimensions of the experience. In this chapter, we will explore strategies for recovery and resilience, empowering individuals to reclaim their sense of self and rebuild their lives in the wake of adversity.

Acknowledging the Pain

The first step in the healing process is acknowledging the pain and trauma that has been inflicted. This requires individuals to confront the reality of their experiences, no matter how painful or overwhelming they may be. By acknowledging the impact of soul murder in the workplace, individuals can begin to validate their own experiences and lay the groundwork for healing.

Seeking Support

One of the most important strategies for healing from workplace trauma is seeking support from trusted friends, family members, or mental health professionals. Talking about one's experiences with others who understand and empathize can provide validation, validation, and support. By reaching out for help, individuals can begin to break the cycle of silence and isolation that often accompanies trauma and take the first steps towards healing.

Cultivating Self-Compassion

Healing from workplace trauma requires individuals to cultivate self-compassion—the ability to treat themselves with kindness, understanding, and empathy. This means acknowledging one's own pain and suffering without judgment or self-blame and recognizing that it is okay to prioritize one's own well-being and needs. By practicing self-compassion, individuals can begin to counteract the negative messages and beliefs that may have been internalized as a result of their experiences.

Establishing Boundaries

Setting and maintaining boundaries is essential for protecting one's physical and emotional well-being in the aftermath of workplace trauma. This may involve setting limits on how much time and energy one devotes to work, saying no to additional responsibilities or demands, or cutting ties with toxic individuals or environments that perpetuate harm. By establishing boundaries, individuals can create a sense of safety and control in their lives and prevent further re-traumatization.

Engaging in Self-Care

Engaging in self-care practices is essential for promoting healing and resilience in the aftermath of workplace trauma. This may involve activities such as exercise, meditation, journaling, or spending time in nature—anything that nourishes the body, mind, and soul and promotes a sense of well-being. By prioritizing self-care, individuals can replenish their energy reserves and build resilience in the face of adversity.

Finding Meaning and Purpose

Finding meaning and purpose in the aftermath of workplace trauma can be a powerful catalyst for healing and growth. This may involve reflecting on one's values, strengths, and goals and identifying ways to align one's life with what truly matters. By finding meaning and purpose, individuals can transcend their experiences of trauma and cultivate a sense of hope, purpose, and resilience in the face of adversity.

Seeking Justice and Accountability

In some cases, healing from workplace trauma may involve seeking justice and accountability for the harm that has been done. This may involve reporting abuse or misconduct to HR or other appropriate authorities, seeking legal recourse through avenues such as workplace harassment or discrimination claims, or advocating for systemic change within the organization. By seeking justice and accountability, individuals can validate their experiences, hold perpetrators accountable for their actions, and prevent further harm from occurring to others.

Embracing Growth and Transformation

Ultimately, healing from workplace trauma is not just about returning to a state of equilibrium—it is about embracing growth and transformation in the aftermath of adversity. This may involve reframing one's experiences as opportunities for learning and growth, finding strength and resilience in the face of challenges, and embracing the journey of self-discovery and self-empowerment. By embracing growth and transformation, individuals can reclaim their sense of agency and authorship over their own lives and emerge from the darkness of trauma into the light of healing and wholeness.

Conclusion

Healing from workplace trauma is a complex and multifaceted process that requires courage, resilience, and support. By acknowledging the pain, seeking support, cultivating self-compassion, establishing boundaries, engaging in self-care, finding meaning and purpose, seeking justice and accountability, and embracing growth and transformation, individuals can begin to reclaim their sense of self and rebuild their lives in the wake of adversity. In the chapters that follow, we will explore strategies and interventions for promoting healing and resilience in the aftermath of workplace trauma, empowering individuals to reclaim their dignity, their humanity, and their souls.

Chapter 8: Breaking the Cycle: Transforming Organizational Culture

In the wake of experiencing soul murder in the workplace, individuals may find themselves not only grappling with their own wounds but also confronting the systemic issues that perpetuate harm within the organization. Transforming organizational culture is essential for preventing future instances of soul murder and creating workplaces that are nurturing, inclusive, and supportive of the well-being of all employees. In this chapter, we will explore strategies for breaking the cycle of toxicity and transforming organizational culture into one that fosters healing, resilience, and growth.

Recognizing the Need for Change

The first step in transforming organizational culture is recognizing the need for change. This requires organizational leaders to acknowledge the reality of workplace trauma and its impact on individuals and the organization as a whole. It also requires a willingness to confront uncomfortable truths and challenge entrenched power dynamics, systems of privilege, and oppressive structures within the organization.

Committing to Transparency and Accountability

Creating a culture of transparency and accountability is essential for promoting trust, integrity, and ethical behavior within the organization. This involves being open and honest with employees about the organization's values, goals, and decision-making processes, and holding leaders and employees alike accountable for their actions and behaviors. By fostering a culture of transparency and accountability, organizations can create an environment where wrongdoing is not tolerated, and where employees feel empowered to speak out against injustice and abuse.

Cultivating Psychological Safety

Psychological safety is the foundation upon which healthy organizational cultures are built. It is the belief that one will not be punished or humiliated for speaking up with ideas, questions, concerns, or mistakes. Creating a culture of psychological safety requires leaders to foster an environment where all voices are valued and respected, where constructive feedback is encouraged, and where mistakes are seen as opportunities for learning and growth. By cultivating psychological safety, organizations can create a climate of trust and collaboration where employees feel empowered to contribute their best work.

Promoting Diversity and Inclusion

Diversity and inclusion are essential for creating workplaces that are equitable, innovative, and resilient. Promoting diversity involves actively recruiting, retaining, and promoting individuals from diverse backgrounds, including those from underrepresented groups. Inclusion involves creating an environment where all employees feel valued, respected, and included, regardless of their race, gender, sexual orientation, or other characteristics. By promoting diversity and inclusion, organizations can harness the full range of perspectives, experiences, and talents of their employees and create a culture of belonging and acceptance.

Empowering Employees

Empowering employees is essential for fostering a sense of ownership, agency, and engagement within the organization. This involves providing employees with the resources, support, and autonomy they need to succeed in their roles and make meaningful contributions to the organization's mission and goals. It also involves recognizing and rewarding employees for their efforts and accomplishments and creating opportunities for professional development and growth. By empowering employees, organizations can create a culture of trust, autonomy, and accountability where employees feel valued and motivated to do their best work.

Investing in Training and Education

Investing in training and education is essential for equipping employees with the knowledge, skills, and tools they need to thrive in a rapidly changing world. This may involve providing training on topics such as diversity and inclusion, conflict resolution, communication skills, and emotional intelligence. It may also involve offering resources such as employee assistance programs, counseling services, and wellness initiatives to support the well-being of employees. By investing in training and education, organizations can create a culture of continuous learning and growth where employees feel supported and empowered to reach their full potential.

Leading by Example

Leadership sets the tone for organizational culture, and leaders must lead by example if they want to create lasting change. This involves modeling the values and behaviors they want to see in others, such as honesty, integrity, empathy, and humility. It also involves being willing to listen to feedback, admit mistakes, and take responsibility for their actions. By leading by example, leaders can inspire trust, confidence, and respect among employees and create a culture of accountability and excellence.

Conclusion

Transforming organizational culture is essential for breaking the cycle of soul murder in the workplace and creating environments that are nurturing, inclusive, and supportive of the well-being of all employees. By recognizing the need for change, committing to transparency and accountability, cultivating psychological safety, promoting diversity and inclusion, empowering employees, investing in training and education, and leading by example, organizations can create a culture of trust, respect, and resilience that promotes healing, growth, and flourishing for all who inhabit it. In the chapters that follow, we will explore strategies and interventions for implementing these principles and creating workplaces that are truly soul-nourishing and life-affirming.

Chapter 9: Holding Accountable: Addressing Perpetrators and Enablers

In the aftermath of soul murder in the workplace, it is crucial to address the individuals responsible for perpetuating harm and creating toxic environments. Holding perpetrators and enablers accountable is essential for promoting justice, preventing future instances of abuse, and creating a culture of integrity and respect within the organization. In this chapter, we will explore strategies for identifying, confronting, and addressing perpetrators and enablers of soul murder in the workplace.

Understanding Perpetrators and Enablers

Perpetrators of soul murder in the workplace are individuals who engage in behaviors that cause harm to others, either through direct actions or through their complicity in creating or maintaining toxic environments. Enablers are individuals who facilitate or condone abusive behavior by failing to intervene or speak out against wrongdoing. Both perpetrators and enablers play a role in perpetuating harm within the organization and must be held accountable for their actions.

Creating a Culture of Accountability

Creating a culture of accountability begins with setting clear expectations for behavior and performance within the organization. This involves establishing codes of conduct, policies, and procedures that define acceptable and unacceptable behavior and outline consequences for violations. It also involves fostering a climate of trust and transparency where employees feel empowered to report misconduct and hold others accountable for their actions. By creating a culture of accountability, organizations can send a clear message that abusive behavior will not be tolerated and that those who engage in it will be held answerable for their actions.

Implementing Fair and Transparent Processes

When addressing allegations of misconduct, it is essential to implement fair and transparent processes that protect the rights of both the accuser and the accused. This may involve conducting thorough investigations, gathering evidence, and interviewing witnesses to determine the facts of the case. It may also involve providing support and resources to those who come forward with allegations of abuse and ensuring that they are protected from retaliation. By implementing fair and transparent processes, organizations can ensure that justice is served and that all parties are treated with dignity and respect.

Holding Perpetrators Accountable

Holding perpetrators accountable for their actions requires taking swift and decisive action to address misconduct and prevent further harm. This may involve imposing disciplinary measures such as warnings, suspensions, or termination of employment, depending on the severity of the offense. It may also involve providing training and counseling to help perpetrators understand the impact of their behavior and learn alternative ways of interacting with others. By holding perpetrators accountable, organizations can send a strong message that abusive behavior will not be tolerated and that there are consequences for violating the rights and dignity of others.

Addressing Enablers

Addressing enablers of soul murder in the workplace is equally important as holding perpetrators accountable. Enablers may include individuals who witness abusive behavior but fail to intervene, managers who turn a blind eye to misconduct, or colleagues who participate in or condone toxic behaviors. Addressing enablers requires creating a culture where speaking out against abuse is encouraged and rewarded, and where bystander intervention is seen as a responsibility rather than an option. By addressing enablers, organizations can disrupt the cycle of abuse and create a culture where everyone feels empowered to speak out against injustice and hold others accountable for their actions.

Providing Support for Victims

In addition to holding perpetrators and enablers accountable, it is essential to provide support and resources for victims of soul murder in the workplace. This may include offering counseling services, legal assistance, or other forms of support to help victims cope with the psychological and emotional toll of abuse. It may also involve creating safe spaces where victims can share their experiences, seek validation and support from others, and access the help they need to heal and recover. By providing support for victims, organizations can demonstrate their commitment to promoting justice and healing for all who have been affected by abuse.

Fostering a Culture of Change

Creating lasting change requires fostering a culture where accountability, integrity, and respect are valued and practiced by all members of the organization. This involves ongoing education and training on topics such as diversity, inclusion, conflict resolution, and ethical leadership. It also involves creating opportunities for dialogue and reflection where employees can discuss their experiences, share their perspectives, and work together to create a more just and equitable workplace. By fostering a culture of change, organizations can create environments where soul murder is not only unacceptable but unthinkable, and where all employees can thrive and flourish.

Conclusion

Holding perpetrators and enablers accountable for their actions is essential for promoting justice, preventing future instances of abuse, and creating a culture of integrity and respect within the organization. By creating a culture of accountability, implementing fair and transparent processes, holding perpetrators and enablers accountable, providing support for victims, and fostering a culture of change, organizations can create environments where soul murder is not tolerated, and where all employees feel safe, valued, and respected. In the chapters that follow, we will explore strategies and interventions for creating cultures of accountability and promoting justice and healing for all who have been affected by abuse.

Chapter 10: Building Support Networks: Finding Allies in Healing

In the aftermath of experiencing soul murder in the workplace, individuals often find themselves grappling with profound feelings of isolation, betrayal, and despair. The journey towards healing and recovery can be daunting, fraught with obstacles and challenges that may seem insurmountable alone. In times of crisis, the importance of building support networks cannot be overstated. These networks, comprised of allies, advocates, and fellow survivors, play a crucial role in providing validation, empathy, and practical assistance to those who have been affected by workplace trauma. In this chapter, we will explore the significance of support networks in the healing process and offer guidance on how to build and leverage these networks effectively.

Understanding the Importance of Support Networks

Support networks serve as a lifeline for individuals who have experienced soul murder in the workplace, offering a sense of belonging, validation, and solidarity in the face of adversity. They provide a safe space where survivors can share their experiences, express their emotions, and seek guidance and support from others who have walked a similar path. Moreover, support networks can offer practical assistance, such as access to resources, information, and advocacy, that can help survivors navigate the challenges of healing and recovery more effectively.

Types of Support Networks

Support networks can take many forms, ranging from informal groups of friends and family members to formal organizations and communities dedicated to supporting survivors of workplace trauma. Some common types of support networks include:

Peer Support Groups: Peer support groups bring together individuals who have experienced similar forms of trauma, providing a space for mutual support, empathy, and understanding. These groups often meet regularly to share their experiences, offer encouragement, and exchange resources and information.

Employee Resource Groups (ERGs): Employee resource groups are formal organizations within the workplace that are dedicated to supporting employees from marginalized or underrepresented groups. These groups may provide advocacy, mentorship, and networking opportunities for survivors of workplace trauma, as well as educational resources and training on topics such as resilience and coping strategies.

Professional Associations: Professional associations and industry-specific organizations may offer support and resources for individuals who have experienced workplace trauma. These associations may provide access to counseling services, legal assistance, and other forms of support that can help survivors navigate the challenges of healing and recovery.

Online Communities: Online communities and forums provide a virtual space where survivors of workplace trauma can connect with others, share their experiences, and access resources and information. These communities may offer anonymity and privacy, making them particularly appealing to individuals who may be hesitant to seek support in person.

Building and Leveraging Support Networks

Building and leveraging support networks requires proactive effort and intentionality on the part of survivors. Here are some strategies for building and leveraging support networks effectively:

Reach Out for Support: Don't be afraid to reach out for support from friends, family members, colleagues, or mental health professionals. Sharing your experiences and emotions with others can help alleviate feelings of isolation and provide validation and empathy.

Seek Out Peer Support Groups: Consider joining a peer support group for survivors of workplace trauma. These groups offer a unique opportunity to connect with others who have walked a similar path and can provide invaluable support and understanding.

Engage with Employee Resource Groups: If your organization has employee resource groups dedicated to supporting survivors of workplace trauma, consider getting involved. These groups may offer a range of resources and support services, as well as opportunities for advocacy and activism within the organization.

Explore Online Communities: Look for online communities and forums where survivors of workplace trauma gather to share their experiences and offer support to one another. These communities can provide a sense of connection and belonging, even if you are unable to access support in person.

Advocate for Change: Consider getting involved in advocacy efforts to raise awareness of workplace trauma and advocate for policies and practices that promote healing and prevention. By speaking out about your experiences and advocating for change, you can help create a more supportive and inclusive workplace culture for all employees.

Conclusion

Building support networks is a critical step in the healing process for survivors of workplace trauma. These networks provide validation, empathy, and practical assistance to individuals who have experienced soul murder in the workplace, helping them navigate the challenges of healing and recovery more effectively. By reaching out for support, engaging with peer support groups and employee resource groups, exploring online communities, and advocating for change, survivors can build strong support networks that foster resilience, empowerment, and healing. In the chapters that follow, we will continue to explore strategies and interventions for supporting survivors of workplace trauma and promoting healing and recovery in the workplace.

Chapter 11: Restoring Purpose and Meaning: Rediscovering Soul in the Workplace

In the wake of experiencing soul murder in the workplace, individuals often find themselves adrift, grappling with profound feelings of disillusionment, despair, and existential emptiness. The trauma inflicted upon them has not only shattered their sense of self and shattered their trust in others but has also stripped away their sense of purpose and meaning in their work. However, amidst the darkness and despair, there lies the possibility of rediscovery—a journey towards reclaiming one's sense of soul and finding meaning and purpose in the workplace once more. In this chapter, we will explore the process of restoring purpose and meaning in the aftermath of workplace trauma and offer guidance on how individuals can rediscover their soul in the workplace.

Understanding the Impact of Workplace Trauma on Purpose and Meaning

Work occupies a central place in many people's lives, providing not only a source of income but also a sense of identity, purpose, and meaning. However, when individuals experience soul murder in the workplace, the trauma inflicted upon them can shatter their sense of purpose and meaning, leaving them feeling lost, disconnected, and adrift. The betrayal of trust, the erosion of dignity, and the existential alienation that often accompany workplace trauma can undermine one's sense of self-worth and rob them of the intrinsic motivation and fulfillment that comes from engaging in meaningful work.

Reconnecting with Values and Beliefs

Restoring purpose and meaning in the workplace begins with reconnecting with one's values, beliefs, and sense of identity. Take time to reflect on what matters most to you, both personally and professionally, and consider how your work aligns with your core values and aspirations. What originally drew you to your chosen field or profession? What aspects of your work bring you joy, fulfillment, and a sense of accomplishment? By rekindling your connection to your values and beliefs, you can begin to rediscover your sense of purpose and meaning in your work.

Finding Meaning in Adversity

While experiencing workplace trauma can be deeply painful and distressing, it can also be an opportunity for growth, resilience, and personal transformation. Many individuals who have experienced soul murder in the workplace report that their ordeal has ultimately led them to reevaluate their priorities, reassess their goals, and rediscover a deeper sense of purpose and meaning in their lives. By reframing adversity as an opportunity for learning and growth, you can begin to find meaning in your experiences and use them as a catalyst for positive change and transformation.

Cultivating Resilience and Adaptability

Restoring purpose and meaning in the workplace requires resilience—the ability to bounce back from adversity and overcome challenges with grace and determination. Cultivate resilience by building a strong support network of friends, family members, colleagues, and mental health professionals who can offer guidance, encouragement, and practical assistance as you navigate the challenges of healing and recovery. Practice self-care techniques such as mindfulness, meditation, and exercise to manage stress, regulate emotions, and foster a sense of inner peace and well-being. Moreover, embrace a growth mindset—the belief that your abilities and intelligence can be developed through effort and perseverance—and approach setbacks and failures as opportunities for learning and growth rather than insurmountable obstacles.

Reimagining Your Relationship with Work

Restoring purpose and meaning in the workplace may also require reimagining your relationship with work and exploring new ways of engaging with your profession or field. Consider how you can leverage your skills, talents, and passions to make a positive impact in your organization, your community, or the world at large. Explore opportunities for growth, development, and self-expression within your current role or consider pursuing new career paths or entrepreneurial ventures that align more closely with your values and aspirations. By approaching your work with curiosity, creativity, and an open mind, you can begin to rediscover the joy, fulfillment, and sense of purpose that comes from engaging in meaningful work.

Conclusion

Restoring purpose and meaning in the workplace is a deeply personal and transformative journey—one that requires courage, resilience, and self-reflection. By reconnecting with your values and beliefs, finding meaning in adversity, cultivating resilience and adaptability, and reimagining your relationship with work, you can begin to rediscover your sense of soul and find purpose and meaning in your work once more. In the chapters that follow, we will continue to explore strategies and interventions for supporting survivors of workplace trauma and promoting healing and recovery in the workplace, so that all individuals can thrive and flourish in their professional lives.

Reclaiming Power: A Case Study of Overcoming Organizational Soul Murder

Case Study: Sally's Journey from Trauma to Triumph

Sally was a highly accomplished professional who had worked her way up to a senior management position in a prestigious agency. She was confident, driven, and passionate about her work. However, upon entering her new role, Sally quickly realized that she had stepped into a toxic environment—one characterized by emotional immaturity, dysfunction, and hostility. Despite her best efforts to lead with compassion and creativity, Sally found herself targeted and tormented by her colleagues, who were resistant to change and threatened by her neurodivergent leadership style.

Recognizing Emotional Triggers

As Sally navigated the challenges of her new role, she began to experience intense feelings of anxiety and depression. She found herself constantly second-guessing her decisions and doubting her abilities. Recognizing that something was amiss, Sally sought out therapy to help her make sense of her experiences and regain control of her mental and emotional well-being.

Understanding the Anatomy of Organizational Trauma

Through therapy, Sally came to understand the profound impact of organizational trauma on her sense of self and identity. She realized that she had been subjected to soul murder in the workplace—a systematic dehumanization and erosion of her dignity and worth. This realization empowered Sally to confront the toxic dynamics within her organization and take steps to protect herself from further harm.

Unmasking Toxic Cultures

With the support of her therapist, Sally began to unmask the signs and symptoms of toxic culture within her organization. She recognized the authoritarian leadership, lack of transparency, and fear-based management tactics that were perpetuating dysfunction and undermining employee well-being. Armed with this knowledge, Sally developed strategies for navigating the toxic dynamics and protecting herself from further harm.

Betrayal and Broken Trust

As Sally delved deeper into her experiences, she came to understand the core of soul murder—betrayal and broken trust. She realized that she had been betrayed by her colleagues and superiors, who had failed to support her and instead undermined her at every turn. This betrayal shattered Sally's confidence and left her feeling isolated and alone.

Power Dynamics and Their Impact

Sally also grappled with the power dynamics at play within her organization. She recognized that those in positions of authority were using their power to maintain the status quo and suppress dissent. This realization fueled Sally's determination to challenge the toxic dynamics and advocate for change within her organization.

The Psychology of Soul Murder

Through therapy, Sally began to explore the psychological roots of soul murder and its impact on individuals. She learned how her irrational beliefs about herself had contributed to her feelings of worthlessness and inadequacy. With the help of her therapist, Sally identified and disputed these beliefs, replacing them with more empowering and affirming thoughts.

Coping Mechanisms for Healing

As Sally worked through her trauma, she developed coping mechanisms to help her navigate the challenges of her workplace. She practiced mindfulness and self-compassion, learning to ground herself in the present moment and cultivate a sense of inner peace and resilience. These coping skills helped Sally to weather the storm and stay focused on her goals.

Building Support Networks

Sally also reached out to her support network for guidance and encouragement. She found allies among her colleagues who shared her concerns about the toxic culture and were willing to stand by her side as she fought for change. Sally also sought support from HR, developing a plan for communicating her experiences and requesting the support she needed to thrive in her role.

Holding Accountable

With the support of her allies and HR, Sally was able to hold her organization accountable for its toxic behavior. She reported the incidents of harassment and discrimination she had experienced and demanded action from senior management. While the agency took steps to address the issues, the damage to Sally's soul was irreparable, and she ultimately made the difficult decision to leave the organization.

Restoring Purpose and Meaning

Despite the trauma she had endured, Sally refused to let her experiences define her. She left the agency and embarked on a journey of self-discovery and renewal. With the support of her therapist and her newfound allies, Sally regained her confidence and reignited her leadership skills. She found purpose and meaning in her work once more, using her experiences to advocate for change and create a more inclusive and supportive work environment.

Conclusion

Sally's journey from trauma to triumph is a testament to the resilience of the human spirit. Despite facing unimaginable challenges and setbacks, Sally refused to be defeated. Through therapy, self-reflection, and the support of her allies, she was able to reclaim her power and rediscover her sense of purpose and meaning in the workplace. While the scars of her experiences may never fully heal, Sally emerged from her ordeal stronger, wiser, and more determined than ever to create positive change in the world around her.

Conclusion: Towards a Future of Wholeness and Well-being

As we come to the conclusion of our exploration into the harrowing phenomenon of soul murder in the workplace, it is imperative to reflect on the lessons learned, the progress made, and the path forward towards a future characterized by wholeness and well-being for all individuals within organizations.

Throughout this journey, we have delved deep into the dark underbelly of organizational dynamics, uncovering the insidious ways in which power imbalances, toxic cultures, and broken trust can inflict profound harm on the human spirit. We have heard the stories of those who have endured soul murder firsthand—their struggles, their traumas, and their resilience in the face of adversity. We have explored the complex interplay of psychological, social, and structural factors that give rise to soul murder, and we have identified strategies and interventions for addressing it at both individual and organizational levels.

One of the most fundamental insights gleaned from our exploration is the recognition that soul murder is not an isolated or rare occurrence, but rather a pervasive and systemic issue that plagues workplaces across industries and sectors. From corporate boardrooms to factory floors, from non-profit organizations to government agencies, no organization is immune to the corrosive effects of toxic cultures and dysfunctional dynamics. However, this recognition is not cause for despair, but rather a call to action—a call to confront the reality of soul murder head-on and to work together towards meaningful change.

Central to our journey towards a future of wholeness and well-being is the concept of healing—not just healing the wounds inflicted by soul murder, but healing the very fabric of our organizations and societies. Healing requires a holistic approach that addresses the root causes of soul murder and fosters a culture of empathy, respect, and compassion within organizations. It requires leadership that is committed to creating environments where individuals feel valued, supported, and empowered to speak out against injustice and abuse. It requires policies and practices that promote equity, inclusion, and diversity, and that hold perpetrators of soul murder accountable for their actions. And perhaps most importantly, healing requires a commitment from all members of the organization—from the C-suite to the front lines—to actively participate in the process of transformation and renewal.

But healing alone is not enough. In order to truly move towards a future of wholeness and well-being, we must also strive for prevention—to identify and address the root causes of soul murder before they have the chance to take hold. This requires a proactive approach that focuses on building resilient and healthy organizations from the ground up—organizations that prioritize the well-being of their employees, that foster a culture of trust and transparency, and that actively work to dismantle systems of oppression and inequality. It requires education and awareness-raising to ensure that all individuals within organizations understand the signs and symptoms of soul murder and feel empowered to take action to prevent it. And it requires ongoing vigilance and commitment from leaders and employees alike to uphold the values of dignity, respect, and integrity in all aspects of organizational life.

As we look towards the future, it is clear that the journey towards wholeness and well-being will not be easy. It will require courage, perseverance, and a willingness to confront uncomfortable truths. It will require us to challenge entrenched power dynamics, to dismantle oppressive systems, and to build new structures and processes that prioritize the humanity and dignity of all individuals within organizations. But it is a journey that is worth taking—a journey towards a future where workplaces are not sites of suffering, but sanctuaries of growth, fulfillment, and flourishing for all who inhabit them.

In closing, let us remember that the fight against soul murder is not a solitary endeavor, but a collective one. It is a fight that requires solidarity, collaboration, and a shared *commitment to creating a world where every individual is valued, respected, and* empowered to reach their full potential. Together, we can build a future where wholeness and well-being are not just aspirational goals, but fundamental rights—and where soul murder in the workplace is nothing more than a distant memory, relegated to the annals of history where it belongs.

www.ingramcontent.com/pod-product-compliance
Lightning Source LLC
Chambersburg PA
CBHW052339220526
45472CB00001B/496